**finding joy
in all
you are**

Other Studies in A Mom's Ordinary Day Bible Study Series

Entering God's Presence
Gaining and Being a Friend
Growing Strong with God
Making Praise a Priority
Managing Your Time
Mothering without Guilt
Winning over Worry

Jean E. Syswerda is mother to three grown children. A former editor and associate publisher at Zondervan, she was responsible for such best-selling Bibles as the *NIV Adventure Bible,* the *NIV Teen Study Bible,* and the *NIV Women's Devotional Bible 1.* She is the general editor of the *NIV Women of Faith Study Bible* and the *NLT Prayer Bible,* as well as the coauthor of the *Read with Me Bible* and the best-selling *Women of the Bible.*

six sessions

YOU & GOD . YOU & OTHERS . YOU & YOUR KIDS

mom

a mom's ordinary day
BIBLE STUDY SERIES

finding joy in all you are

JEAN E. SYSWERDA
general editor

written by
JEAN E. SYSWERDA

GRAND RAPIDS, MICHIGAN 49530 USA

ZONDERVAN™

Finding Joy in All You Are
Copyright © 2003 by Jean Syswerda

Requests for information should be addressed to:
Zondervan, *Grand Rapids, Michigan 49530*

ISBN 0-310-24712-8

All Scripture quotations, unless otherwise indicated, are taken from the *Holy Bible: New International Version*®. NIV®. Copyright © 1973, 1978, 1984 by International Bible Society. Used by permission of Zondervan. All rights reserved.

Scripture quotations marked THE MESSAGE are taken from *The Message,* Copyright © 1993, 1994, 1995, 1996, 2000, 2001, 2002. Used by permission of NavPress Publishing Group.

Scripture quotations marked NLT are taken from the *Holy Bible, New Living Translation,* copyright © 1996. Used by permission of Tyndale House Publishers, Inc., Wheaton, Illinois 60189. All rights reserved.

All rights reserved. No part of this publication may be reproduced, stored in a retrieval system, or transmitted in any form or by any means—electronic, mechanical, photocopy, recording, or any other—except for brief quotations in printed reviews, without the prior permission of the publisher.

Interior design by Tracey Moran

Printed in the United States of America

03 04 05 06 07 08 09 /❖ CH/ 10 9 8 7 6 5 4 3 2 1

contents

7   how to use this study guide
11 introduction
17 session 1: you are . . . you
27 session 2: you are . . . mom
35 session 3: you are . . . wife
45 session 4: you are . . . friend
55 session 5: you are . . . family
65 session 6: you are . . . beautiful
77 leader's notes

how to use this study guide

Hey, Mom, are you ready?

When was the last time you did something just for you? In the joy and junk and memories and mess that is your life as a mother, do you sometimes feel that you've lost something—something essential and important?

The Bible studies in this series will help you rediscover and, even more, enjoy all the parts and pieces that make you a unique person, a unique mother, and a unique and holy creation of God.

The five sections of each individual session are designed to meet a particular need in your life—the need for time alone, for time with God's Word, for time with others, for time with God, and for time with your children. How you approach and use each section is up to you and your individual styles and desires. But here are a few suggestions:

For You Alone

The operative word here is, of course, *alone*. For moms who rarely even go to the bathroom alone, being alone can seem an almost impossible goal. Perhaps thinking in terms of *quiet* would help. You can do this part of the study in any quiet moments in your home—when kids are sleeping, when they're watching a video, when you're nursing a little one. Any quiet or personal time you can find in your own schedule will work. This part of the study is sometimes serious, sometimes fun, sometimes downright silly. It will prepare your mind for the other sections of the study.

For You and God's Word

Put this study guide, a pen, and your Bible in a favorite place—somewhere you can grab it at any free moment, perhaps in the kitchen or by a favorite chair. Then, when a few spare moments arise, everything you need is right at hand. Each of the six sessions includes a short Bible study for you to complete alone. (This doesn't necessarily mean you have to *be* alone to complete it! My daughter reads her Bible out loud during a morning bath while her infant son sits in his bouncy seat next to her. She gets her Bible read, and he's content with the sound of his mommy's voice.)

For You and Others

The third section of each study is intended for small groups (even just two is a small group!), but if that isn't possible, you *can* complete it alone. Or connect with a friend or neighbor to work through the materials together. If you function as the leader, little preparation is required; you can learn right along with your fellow mothers. The leader is actually more of a facilitator, keeping the discussion on track and your time together moving along. Leadership information on many of the questions in the "For You and Others" section is included at the back of this book, beginning on page 77.

For You and God

The fourth section of each session will guide you in a time of prayer based on the study's topic. Wonder when you'll find time to do this? Prop this book up in your window while doing dishes. God hears the prayers of moms whose hands are in dishwater! Or take it along in the car when picking up a child from an activity. Or use it while nursing an infant. These times of talking to God are precious moments in the life of a mom. And with all the demands on your time, you need to grab these moments whenever you can. Do also try, though, to find a time each day for quiet, concentrated prayer. Your children need their mom to be "prayed up" when she faces each day.

For You and Your Kids

How great is this? A Bible study that includes something for your kids as well as for you! The final section of each session gives suggestions on applying the principles of the study in your kids' lives as well as in your own. The activities are appropriately geared to different ages and range from simple to more complex.

One Important Final Note

Don't presume you have to move through these sessions in any particular order. The order in which they appear in each study is the ideal. Life doesn't always allow the ideal, however. If you start your study with the last section and then go through from back to front, you'll still be fine. Do whatever works best for you and your schedule and for your treasured little (or not-so-little) offspring.

introduction

Mommy, Mommy! Read me a book.
    Let's play a game.
        Can I go outside?
Where are you?
        Sing me a song.
I need a hug.
Mom! Mom! Did you sign my permission slip?
    I don't want PBJ in my lunch. Gross!
        Can I go over to my friend's house after school?
            Do I have to ride the bus again today?
Where are my shoes?
Mother! Are you home?
    Where are my books?
        Is supper ready yet?
            What time do I have to be at church tonight?
Did anyone call me today?
Hey! Mom!
    Can I borrow the car?
        Where's my basketball?
            I have to leave for work right now!
    Can I stay out an hour later tonight?

Everyone wants a piece of mom.

Little ones need help. School-age kids need direction. Teens need encouragement. And everyone needs to know where their shoes ended up.

The demands of motherhood can make a mom forget who she is *besides* a mom—who she is as a whole person.

Wife
    Friend
        Family member
            Beautiful person
                Believer

This study on *Finding Joy in All You Are* will help a mom discover more about herself—who she is as a mom, as a believer, and as a unique creation of God—and how to make her life one of purpose, balance, and beauty.

Each of the six sessions focuses on one aspect of you as a person:

🌸 **session 1: you are . . . you**
You are a unique creation of God—his treasured possession.

🌸 **session 2: you are . . . mom**
No denying it. This "you" consumes most of your energy and time. Be the best you can be at it!

🌸 **session 3: you are . . . wife**
A fresh look at a much-maligned word: submission. You submit every day—to your children and their needs, to God (Jesus submitted, too), to schedules, to bosses, and to your husband.

🌸 **session 4: you are . . . friend**
What would you do without good friends? This session emphasizes the importance of friendship in the life of a mom.

🌸 **session 5: you are . . . family**
Discover the importance of family—your immediate family as well as your extended family. They are an integral part of who you are.

🌸 **session 6: you are . . . beautiful**
You are! Your hair may not be cut in the latest style. Maybe your nose isn't the fashionable length. You may not be the best home decorator or cook. But you're still a beautiful, wonderful, treasured creation before the only one who really counts: God.

Juggling all the parts and pieces that make up the life of a mother can strain the ability of even the most talented. The demands on her time—not to mention the demands on her emotions—put the strongest women flat on the floor at times.

Perhaps while going through this study, moms will discover that flat on the floor isn't always the worst place to be. For it is there—when you're at your weakest and most vulnerable—that God can do his best work in you.

You're invited to buckle up and take a ride through the twists and turns that make up your life. We pray that through each session you'll discover more about yourself—and more about the God who created you.

a mom's ordinary day

finding joy in all
you are

> *Therefore, if anyone is in Christ, [she] is a new creation; the old has gone, the new has come!*
>
> 2 Corinthians 5:17

session 1

you are . . . you

 ## For You Alone

Let's start this session with some contemplation. Turn your mind inward as you think about who you are as an individual. Here's a little acrostic to help you get started:

      I   A M   M E

Under each letter write at least one word that describes who you are. For example, one of the "Ms" would likely be *mom.* "E" could be *enthusiastic* or *entertaining* or *expert.* For "I," think of words like *introspective* and *insecure* and *intense.* Don't let the acrostic confine you. You don't necessarily have to add only words that fit neatly into it.

Now turn your sights away from yourself and the acrostic and look to God. Who are you in him? What sort of relationship do you have with him? How does this relationship affect who you are?

Being a mother can quickly eclipse all the other great things you are as a person. Without attention to your other parts and pieces, the task of sorting out who you are other than *mother* can become more and more difficult. The most important person you are is in your status as a believer. This first study will help you review and recall that significant part of you as a person.

 ## For You and God's Word

Begin your study today by reading 2 Corinthians 5:17. As you read this verse, take every word personally. Read it as though Paul is writing to you personally about your relationship with God, about who you now are as a believer in Jesus Christ.

> *Therefore, if anyone is in Christ, [she] is a new creation; the old has gone, the new has come!*
>
> 2 CORINTHIANS 5:17

"If I belong to Christ and believe in him, I am a new person; the old me is gone, the new me has come!" That's a paraphrase of 2 Corinthians 5:17. Here are a few questions to get you thinking about what this verse means for you personally:

1. What does it mean to you to be "in Christ" in a spiritual sense?

2. What practical implications, if any, does being "in Christ" have?

3. How does or, perhaps more realistically, *should* being "in Christ" affect your day-to-day life?

4. What is your most common response when the "old you" rears its (sometimes) ugly head? If you understood all the richness of this verse, what sort of response would you be encouraged to make?

5. Only in and through Christ can you ever become all God created you to be. Who are you as a person in Christ—as a "new creation"? Complete at least four "I am" statements below to help you see yourself in a more holistic way. Here are a few ideas to help you get going:

   - I am creative.

   - I am passionate.

   - I am a good listener.

   - I am _____.

   - I am _____.

   - I am _____.

   - I am _____.

For You and Others

As a small group, you gather to examine Scripture and who you are as a person in light of Scripture. Today's passages will give you insight, guiding your thoughts and your talk and helping you recognize what you once were and now are in Christ.

> *If you are in Christ, you are a new creation; the old has gone, the new has come!*
>
> 2 CORINTHIANS 5:17 (paraphrased)

Recite this verse together as a group, then discuss the following questions:

1. Share with each other what being "in Christ" means to you personally.

2. Share what you discovered spiritually and practically about this phrase in "For You and God's Word."

Forgiveness (past sins)

Now turn to Ephesians 2:13, which speaks of being "near" and "far away" because of your position "in Christ."

3. Near what? Far away from what?

Near God.

4. How do you go from being far away to being near?

Having a relationship
"Know your face"

5. What does being near mean when you are doing the everyday things of life? How does it affect your life when you're preparing meals? Driving children around? Cleaning your home? Getting home from work yourself or welcoming your husband home?

Taking God out of a "box" when you chat as you go through life. Headset with God. Recharge batteries through the Word.

6. When do you find yourself feeling most near to God? Most far away?

   Near — when doing His will
   Church
   Far — yelling at children
   Kids crying

7. What might help you stay near God more of the time?

   Christian friends
   Letting Him participate

Carefully read together 2 Corinthians 4:7–18.

8. Why do you think Paul likens you to a clay jar?

9. What is the treasure he speaks of?

10. How are you "wasting away"? Physically? Emotionally? Mentally? Other ways?

Not staying healthy through excercise and nutrition.

11. Those are outward things. What's happening to you inwardly because you are "in Christ"?

Isaiah 40:31 – soar like an eagle

12. Describe what sort of "light and momentary troubles" you're experiencing right now.

13. Where does Paul tell you to fix your eyes?

Jesus

SESSION ONE: YOU ARE ...YOU 23

14. How does fixing your eyes on Jesus help you discover the person you really are?

He is the creator

15. How does fixing your eyes on your situation cloud your discovery of the person you really are?

16. Take your list of "I am's" from "For You and God's Word" and make a new list together. This is a list of becomings:

- I am becoming _____.
- I am becoming _____.
- I am becoming _____.

When you think too little (or too much!) of yourself, you're belittling God's very creation. So, instead, give him the glory and celebrate all you have become and are becoming in him.

God loves you enough to keep working on you, making you everything he intended you to be when he created you. All your parts and pieces—physical, mental, emotional—are part of his design. If you look at yesterday, you may think you haven't become

much of a new creation. Look instead at what you were a year ago—
or several years ago—and celebrate the progress you've made.

Close your time together as a small group with a celebration.
You are not what you used to be.
Praise God!
You are not all that you will become.
Praise God!

 **For You and God**

Many of the people in your life define you by only one or two parts of the whole you. They may know you as mom. Or as someone's wife. Or as the cleaning lady. Or as an artist or teacher or good cook or singer. A few people in your life know you more intimately. But no one on this earth will ever know you fully and completely. That's a fact of life. All your parts and pieces, all your quirks and qualities, all the depth of your entire personality—no one person will ever be intimately acquainted with all of it.

But never fear, there *is* someone who knows you thoroughly and completely.

The end of Paul's love chapter (1 Corinthians 13) talks about how you may not see much of anything clearly right now. But it ends with the wonderful assurance that, though you don't know everything fully—including yourself—you are fully known by God.

Find a quiet place (not easy for moms of busy children!) to read 1 Corinthians 13. As you spend time meditating, thank God for these words in verse 12: "I am fully known."

 **For You and Your Kids**

Preschool–Elementary

Sit down with your children and ask each one to draw a picture of his or her face. You draw a picture of your own face also. After the pictures are completed, look at them and talk about them. Why this color or that color? Why happy or sad?

Share with your children what their pictures tell you. Be sure to go beyond the physical features and focus on their *being*—who they are more than what they look like. (For example, "The big smile you drew shows me you're a happy person.") Let them share what your picture tells them about you. Encourage them by talking with them about the best parts of their personalities.

Middle–High School

Ask your children to make their own list of their roles in life and their personality traits, using the "I ... AM ... ME" acrostic if you wish (see page 17). Talk together about their list. Help them discover their good points and deal with their negative reactions or things they're not very good at. Encourage them to share their feelings about themselves, whether positive or negative.

All Ages

Offer assurance of your love and God's love for your children. Above all, help them see that God created them as unique and special. Encourage them to ask God to help them continue to grow and become all he wants them to be.

session 2

you are . . . mom

 For You Alone

Let's start off with a little quiz to help you assess where you are. Just check the appropriate boxes. If the statement doesn't apply to you, leave the box blank.

- ❑ I have children under five years old.
- ❑ I have children over five years old.
- ❑ I have more than one teenager.
- ❑ I have a husband who consistently works more than fifty hours a week.
- ❑ I have clean dishes in the dishwasher and dirty dishes in the sink.
- ❑ I have dirty dishes in the dishwasher, the sink, under the table . . .
- ❑ I haven't gone to the bathroom alone for at least one month.
- ❑ My car has at least one McDonald's toy or French fry under the seat.
- ❑ I have been called out of church to the nursery at least once in the last year.
- ❑ I have more than one child who has to be more than one place at the same time today.
- ❑ I think spaghetti *with hot dogs* is not only a nourishing meal but borders on refined cuisine.

- ❏ My teenager has rolled his or her eyes at me at least once already today.
- ❏ My husband looks at me with astonishment when I tell him what I cleaned up today.
- ❏ I am more likely to respond when my friend's kids call me "mom" than when my friend herself calls me by my given name.
- ❏ I have a name besides "Mom," but I don't think I remember it.
- ❏ I am more likely to find small pieces of candy in my couch than money.
- ❏ I know more about proper baby-burping techniques than I ever knew about one aspect of my business before I had children.

If you checked more than ten of these boxes, you are a prime candidate for a case (at least some of the time) of mommy-itis.

Make no mistake. You love being a mom and all the particular and peculiar pieces of your life that go with it. Your children are your dream and your mission in life right now. Even so, at times being a mom is hard work. And overwhelming. And intense and draining. This study will help you gain new focus and enthusiasm for your important role as *mother*.

 ## For You and God's Word

> The Christian mother must turn a deaf ear to the babble
> of voices vying for her attention and listen to God.
> It is in Scripture that she will find the only safe
> and reliable information about how to fulfill
> her calling as a wife and mother.
>
> BARBARA BUSH, *MASTERING MOTHERHOOD*

The word *mother* appears over three hundred times in the Bible. God obviously considers it one of life's most significant roles. Most of the wisdom in Scripture regarding mothering is found in the stories and insights of mothers as they relate to their children. However, one passage in particular (Proverbs 31:10–31) does give a generous poetic picture of a wife and mother. Many women can't read this passage of Scripture without feeling guilty for what they're not. Don't fall into this trap.

Find a quiet moment to prayerfully read this passage with two primary thoughts in mind:

- How am I already like the woman described here?

- How am I *not* like the woman described here?

Don't waste time worrying about what you aren't and never will be. Instead, look for areas where growth is possible and even necessary. Keep your focus on verse 28—that in time a job well-done will win the praise of your children.

 ## For You and Others

Many bright, capable women—leaders of corporations and classrooms—collapse into a jumble of tears and insecurities when faced with the rigors of mothering. Why? Probably because of the eternal significance of the task, as well as the piece of your heart each of your children carries. As you study together today, do your best to put on an honest face, sharing not only the joys but also the difficulties you face as mothers.

Read 1 Samuel 1:1-28 and 1 Samuel 2:18-21. As a group, ponder this story of sacrificial motherhood.

1. 1 Samuel 1:3-8 describes the reactions to infertility of three people—Hannah, Peninnah, and Elkanah. If anyone in your group has struggled with infertility, ask her to share, if she is willing, the reality of each of these reactions—what is good, bad, ugly, or hard about each one.

SESSION TWO: YOU ARE ... MOM   29

2. Read verses 9–18. Compare Hannah's *reaction* to her infertility (verse 7) with her *response* to her infertility (verse 10). What makes it hard to go from merely reacting to responding?

3. When have you prayed with such intensity that someone seeing you might have thought you were drunk (verses 12–14)? What were you praying for? How did God answer your prayer?

4. When Hannah's husband told her to cheer up, she didn't (verse 8), but when the priest, Eli, told Hannah to cheer up, she did (verses 17–18). What made the difference? Why do you think Hannah put so much faith in what Eli told her?

5. Read verses 19-28. Verses 19 and 20 say that the Lord "remembered" Hannah and gave her a child. Had he forgotten her? What is meant by "remembered" here?

Faithful and obedient

6. Hannah made a promise (verse 11), remembered her promise (verse 22), then kept her promise (verse 24). How does God express his desire that you keep his promises? What promises have you made to others—your children, your husband, your extended family? How have you kept those promises? How important is it that you keep your promises? Why?

Promise to marry & stay together

7. Picture yourself in the scene in verses 26-28, as Hannah brought Samuel to the temple, worshiped there, then left him there. Describe your feelings.

8. How old do you think Samuel was?

   Three or four

9. Why do you think Hannah decided to fulfill her promise at this particular time?

   He was weaned

10. Mothering still involves hard choices today. What hard things have you had to do as a mother? Where do you find support for those times?

11. Read 1 Samuel 2:18–21 again. Imagine Hannah sewing a coat—a bit larger each year—for Samuel. What might she have been thinking as she sewed? What sort of tasks do you do for your children that, if you take the time to think about it, are as loving and carefully executed as Hannah's sewing? What could you be doing for your children *as* you take care of these tasks?

Without a doubt, mothering is one of the most sacrificial roles on earth. With each child you give a bit more of your heart and yourself away. But it can also be one of the most rewarding roles on earth. As you close your session today, talk about a few of the rewards of mothering that you've experienced recently.

 ## For You and God

Use Luke 1:46–55 (the song of Jesus' mother, Mary—one of the most revered mothers of all time) for your prayer today. You can pray these words to God just as they appear in your Bible, or you can put the thoughts into your own words. Either way, thank God for his work in your life as you mother the children he has given you.

 ## For You and Your Kids

Preschool–Lower Elementary

Draw a simple, large happy face and a simple, large sad face. Talk to your little ones about things that make you happy and things that make you sad as a mom. Encourage them to tell you about what makes them happy and what makes them sad as they relate to you as their mother.

Upper Elementary–High School

Make a list of the following phrases for you and your kids to complete:

- I wish you would_____.
- I wish you wouldn't _____.
- I'm glad you _____.

After you've completed these sentences, talk about them together. Be ready for honest input, and take it seriously. Look your children in the eyes as they share with you. Then share with them what you wrote. If possible, make one of your answers silly (I wish you would spill milk more often; I wish you wouldn't make your bed so willingly each morning)—just to keep things a bit lighthearted.

All Ages

One of life's best activities is to *pray with* your kids. It's amazing how quickly annoyances, irritations, problems, and tensions with your kids fade when you pray with them. Commit to not only praying for your kids but with them on a regular basis, perhaps at a meal or just as they leave for school or go to bed. The time you do it doesn't matter, but the act itself can have eternal benefits.

session 3

you are . . . wife

 For You Alone

Rate these communications with your husband from 1 to 10 in their order of importance:

_____ Please pick up your socks.

_____ I love you.

_____ Don't forget to stop at the store on your way home.

_____ You're a great dad.

_____ When you sing in the shower [or something else], it makes me happy.

_____ You're a great husband.

_____ Would you do the dishes tonight?

_____ I need you.

_____ You work/golf/hunt/_____ way too much.

_____ The kids drove me nuts today.

Now put them in order (be honest!) of the frequency with which you use them. Relationships are made up of all the little communications of day-to-day living. The communications that make relationships significant, however, can get lost in the busyness of each day. Look through the list again. What important things haven't you said to your husband lately?

For You and God's Word

Are you ready? For this study and the next, you'll wrestle with two passages of Scripture that deal with that word many women only want to whisper: *shhhhh, submission.* Turn to Paul's letter to the Colossians:

> *Wives, understand and support your husbands by submitting to them in ways that honor the Master. Husbands, go all out in love for your wives. Don't take advantage of them.*
>
> COLOSSIANS 3:18–19 THE MESSAGE

Try to read these two verses with a mind open to what God has to say to you about your relationship with your husband. For some women, submitting isn't an issue. For others, it's a difficulty. Some women have husbands who don't love them or who treat them harshly. Others have loving and kind mates. Each woman's situation and her reactions to it are different.

After you've read these verses several times (perhaps in several different Bible versions), think about these questions:

1. Why is submitting to your husband difficult (if it is)? Is the problem within you? Or within him?

Examples in men that I grew up with were not ideal. Before I understood he needs to be walking w/ God, was difficult. Not a big problem today. Sort of nice at times. Less pressure on me.

2. What would a loving submission in your particular marriage look like? What sort of results would it bring?

    Less cautious.

3. What can you do to encourage your husband to *want* to go all out for you? Show him my love for God and His word. Show how I respect his judgement.

4. In what way does (or has) your husband take advantage of you (or, as the NIV states, is harsh with you)? Is there anything you can do about it?

5. In what way have you not made it a priority to understand and support your husband? Why? And what can you do about it?

   Some of his new business and ministry ideas. Too cautious because of life experience & my nature.

If you tend to dismiss these verses, thinking that they're only an illustration of the chauvinistic culture of Paul's day, you'll miss a vital truth of Christianity. Submission runs counter to our culture. So does the servant attitude expressed by Jesus (see John 13:1–17; Philippians 2:3–8) and expected of those who follow him (see Ephesians 5:21).

6. The whole submission issue becomes a *non-issue* when a husband and wife treat each other with respect and love. If respect and love in your home are in short supply, however, the only thing you can do about it is change something about yourself. You can't change your husband. You can only change *you*. How does that thought affect how you approach the issue of submission?

For You and Others

Read Ephesians 5:21-33.

1. Begin your discussion by defining submission. What does it mean? What does it look like in marriage?

2. Why do you think submission has gotten such a tarnished image?

   Women's rights movement. Men who aren't walking w/Christ want women to submit to their ways.

3. Who is doing the submitting in each of these verses?
   - Ephesians 5:21 __Christians__
   - Ephesians 5:22 __wives__
   - Ephesians 5:24 __church, wives__
   - Romans 13:1, 5 __Citizens__
   - 1 Corinthians 16:15-16 __Converts to Christ__

- Hebrews 5:7 _Jesus_
- 1 Peter 2:18 _slaves_
- 1 Peter 3:22 _angels authorities & powers_
- 1 Peter 5:5 _young_

4. Name some people or groups to whom you as a woman submit. Now name some people or groups to whom your husband submits.

   Parents, children

   Terry- work, family, church

5. To whom does Paul call all believers to submit (Ephesians 5:21, 24)? _Christ_

6. Describe submission in terms of *giving in* or *giving up*. Then describe submission in terms of living *selflessly*. Which is easier to swallow? Why? Which type of submission do you think Paul has in mind here?

   Living selflessly is easier

> *If we all willingly and lovingly put others before self, submission becomes a non-issue. What a transformation such selflessness would make in a marriage, in a home, in the church!*
>
> NIV WOMEN OF FAITH STUDY BIBLE

7. If a wife is called to submit, what does Paul call husbands to do in this passage? How many times does he tell them to do it? Is there any significance in the number of reminders?

8. What sort of love is described in verse 25?

Sacrificial love.

> *In the married relationship, the beginning of the equation is not submission, but love. A husband's loving interaction with his wife will produce a willing submission to him. A wife's loving interaction with her husband will produce tender leadership on his part.*
>
> NIV WOMEN OF FAITH STUDY BIBLE

9. So the crux of the issue is that you all submit to

   _____ . And you all submit to

   _____ .

Let's try to shun the incorrect emphasis often taken from this passage that wives are the only ones submitting. In essence, Paul calls *everyone* to submit to each other and to Christ. Husbands in their loving leadership submit to their wives. And wives in their loving selflessness submit to their husbands. That's the scriptural approach to submission. As we get down to real life, though, we need to see what submission looks like in a home.

10. Describe a particular situation in which you would be called to submit to your husband.

Job decisions

11. Describe a particular way in which your husband might submit to you.

    Spending time w/ kids vs. a guy outing.

12. How does prayer fit into the submission equation? What effect might praying about it (or not praying about it) have on your attitude?

    Prayer changes attitudes.
    Pray for husbands submission to Christ.

Just as Christ was intensely and yet humbly submissive to the Father, you can be intensely and yet humbly submissive to your husband. This doesn't imply checking your opinions or your brains at the door. It just means lovingly putting others before self—which is exactly what Christ did for you.

For You and God

Spend time today contemplating the word *submit*. In your prayers, follow the steps listed below, taking one step at a time—not moving to the next until you're completely ready:

- Ask God to help you leave behind the bitterness, the hurt, or the anger that thoughts of submission sometimes stir up.
- Ask God to replace these negative attitudes with love for your husband, as well as for all the others to whom you must submit.

- Ask God to change your perspective from worrying about your own place and your own rights to selflessly putting others before yourself. Ask him to help you see that you can still be strong and creative.
- Tell God about the times you have difficulty submitting, and ask him to change your heart.

> Submission doesn't mean women become wimpy, doormat wives. Submission requires an inner strength to obey God and willingly submit to one's husband. It means finding fulfillment and esteem in the godly role of wife.
>
> NIV WOMEN OF FAITH STUDY BIBLE

For You and Your Kids

All Ages

Play the submission game. Everyone gets a chance to be in charge, with all the others submitting to him or her. You start out as the one in charge in order to set the tone for the game. Tell your kids they have to do whatever you tell them. Think of the silliest things you can: bark like a dog, run like a chicken, make the silliest face possible, pretend you're on a scary carnival ride—whatever you can come up with. All the others must "submit" to you. After a few moments, let the others be in charge while you submit. Whatever they tell you to do (within reason, of course), you must submit.

When everyone tires of the game, sit together and discuss the concept of submission. You can use the following questions to spark conversation:

- What did you like better—being the one who had to submit or being the one in charge? Why?

- When is submission hard? When might it be easy?

session 4

you are . . . friend

For You Alone

Over the years, the TV show *Friends* has gained an almost cultic following. While the show may not always model the kind of proper and upright living you'd like it to, it does showcase friendship in a way that few others have attempted over the years. Whether you watch it regularly or have never watched it, tune in to one of the episodes and work through the following questions:

What kinds of friendships do the women in the show have?

What kinds of friendships do the men have?

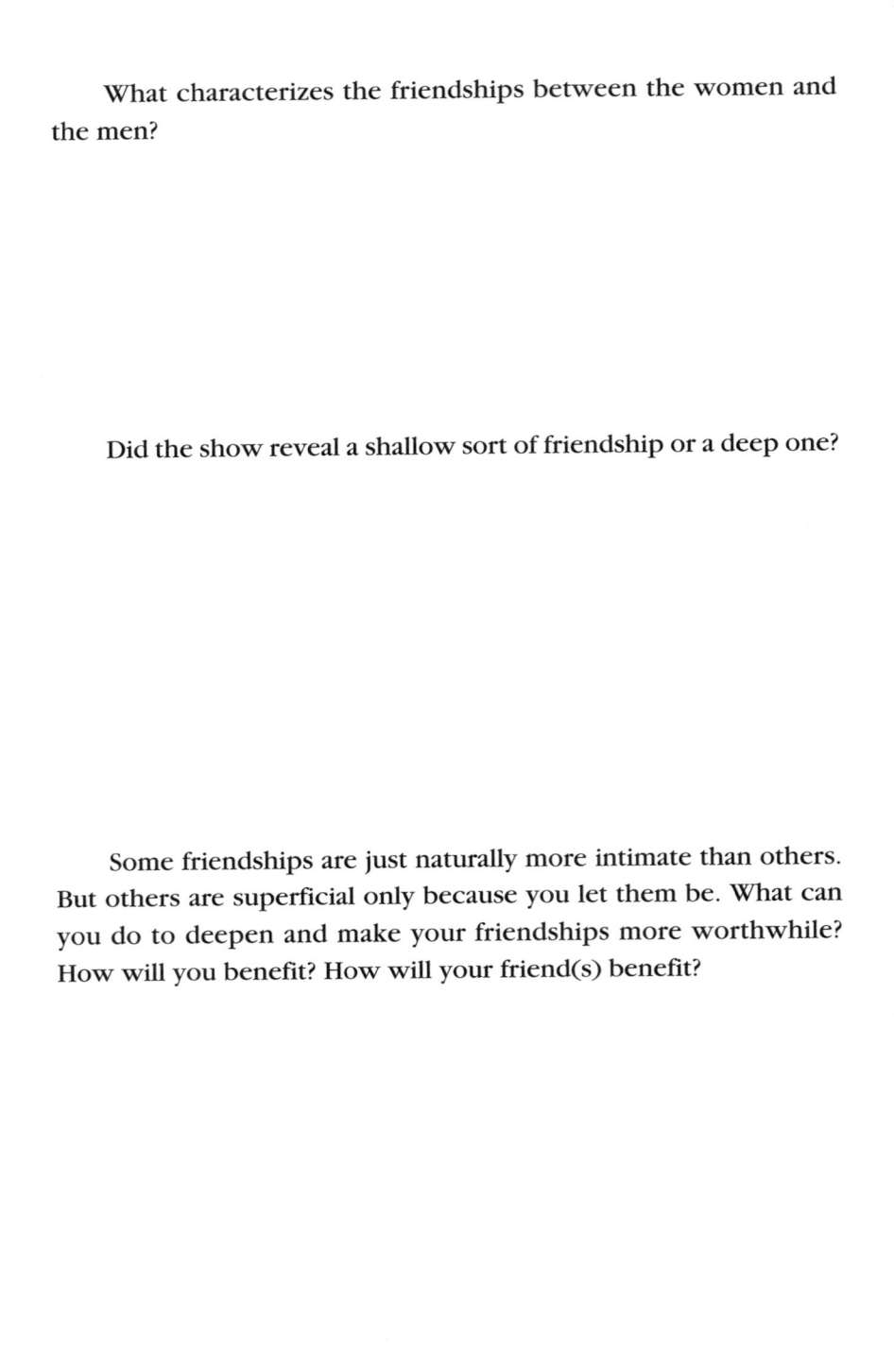

What characterizes the friendships between the women and the men?

Did the show reveal a shallow sort of friendship or a deep one?

Some friendships are just naturally more intimate than others. But others are superficial only because you let them be. What can you do to deepen and make your friendships more worthwhile? How will you benefit? How will your friend(s) benefit?

For You and God's Word

> *It's better to have a partner than go it alone.*
> *Share the work, share the wealth.*
> *And if one falls down, the other helps,*
> *But if there is no one to help, tough!*
>
> *Two in a bed warm each other.*
> *Alone, you shiver all night.*
>
> *By yourself you're unprotected.*
> *With a friend you can face the worst.*
> *Can you round up a third?*
> *A three-stranded rope isn't easily snapped.*
>
> ECCLESIASTES 4:9–12 THE MESSAGE

1. Begin your time today by bringing to mind the people you think of as your friends. Think of the one or two people you consider to be your closest friends. What similarities in character and interests do you share? What differences?

2. How does this passage accurately describe your friendship? How is it not accurate?

3. What is the most important facet of friendship included in this passage?

4. What is the most important facet of your relationship with your friend(s)?

5. Perhaps you don't make friends easily or you consider yourself to be a bit of a loner. What might you be missing if you don't have close friends?

> *One mother, whose two children are almost grown, summarized what mother after mother told me when she said, "The most helpful thing I ever found for dealing with my stress as a mother was my friendships with other mothers. I wish as a young mother I had taken more time to develop friendships. I don't know why I didn't. Maybe I was just too wrapped up in the newness and the stress of young children. But I didn't learn until later how important such friendships are.*
>
> DEBORAH SHAW LEWIS, *MOTHERHOOD STRESS*

6. How do your friends help you as you fill your role as a mother?

For You and Others

> *The glory of friendship is not the outstretched hand, nor the kindly smile, nor the joy of companionship; it is the spiritual inspiration that comes to one when he discovers that someone else believes in him and is willing to trust him with his friendship.*
>
> RALPH WALDO EMERSON

The book of Proverbs offers many valuable morsels of advice on friendship—not just what friendship is but what you can do to be a good friend. With a few others (some will likely be your friends!), travel through the friendship passages of Proverbs. Fill in the blanks together, then discuss the answers to the questions.

- **Read Proverbs 12:26.**

The NIV states that a righteous person will be _____ in her friendships.

Why would or should this proverb be true?

Talk about a time when a friend hurt you. What happened to your friendship?

Talk about a time when a friend helped you. What happened to your friendship?

> *A simple friend thinks the friendship over when you have an argument. A real friend knows that it's not a friendship until after you've had a fight.*
>
> UNKNOWN

- **Read Proverbs 16:28.**

    Close friends can be separated by _____ .
    How would you define gossip?

    Why does it do so much damage?

- **Read Proverbs 17:9.**

    What do good friends do for each other? Why would you do this?

Describe a time when you think it might be better to confront your friend with her failings rather than overlook them. What risks do you take then with your friendship?

- **Read Proverbs 17:17.**

    A true friend loves
    - a. some of the time.
    - b. most of the time.
    - c. all the time.

    Describe some situations when loving your friends *all the time* may be difficult. If it's difficult, why would you choose to do it?

- **Read Proverbs 27:6.**

  _____ from a friend can be trusted.

Really?

What sort of wounds have your friends given you? What sort of wounds have you inflicted on your friends?

To close your time together as a small group, turn to the person on your left and share one thing about her that you think would make her a good friend.

For You and God

In John 15:12-14 Jesus calls "friends" all who love each other and do as he commands. What about your lifestyle could harm your friendship with God? What do you do or what kind of character traits do you have that may make you a better friend of God?

Talk to God today as you would talk to a friend, just as Moses did in the desert (Exodus 33:11). Think of how easily and intimately you can talk with a close friend. Talk to God the same way, sharing your needs, concerns, and praises.

For You and Your Kids

Preschool–Lower Elementary

Sit down with paper and paints or markers. Give each child a large piece of paper and markers or brushes. Encourage them to think about one friend and what they like about this friend's face.

It will tell you something about what this friendship means to them. You do the same: Think about one of your friends and what you like about her face. Then together draw your friends' faces, talking the whole time about having and being good friends.

Upper Elementary–High School

Discuss friendship with your children. Encourage them (by talking about your own friendships) to think about their friends—especially their close friends—and what these friends have contributed to their lives. Using just regular paper or special stationery, write thank-you notes to your friends.

All Ages

Talk together about what it means to have a friend and what it means to *be* a friend. Plan something you can do for your friends to show your appreciation.

session 5

you are . . . family

For You Alone

Extended family can be either a blessing or a bother. Sometimes they're both all at once. On a sheet of paper, list the members of your extended family with whom you have regular contact (if you live away from your extended family, think of *family* in terms of close friends, older people who fill in as grandparents to your children, and so forth). Next to each name write the first characteristic for each that comes to mind. Here are some ideas: kind, silly, compassionate, passionate, talkative, quiet, depressed, happy, quirky, hippie, sweet, opinionated, strong, talented.

When you finish, look over the list. What kind of mix of people do you have in your family? Many the same? Many different? Who is the natural leader of your family? How do you know he or she is the leader? Is that leadership a good thing? A not-so-good thing?

Now write your own name across the bottom of the list and write one characteristic for yourself. How do you (or perhaps you don't) fit into the mix that is your family?

> *Some family trees bear an enormous crop of nuts.*
> WAYNE H.

For You and God's Word

Families formed the most integral part of society in Bible times. Every other social function revolved around the family unit.

But family back then had a larger context than what we think of today. Two and even three generations lived together in one household as a family. Children grew up closely surrounded by not only their immediate family but also their aunts, uncles, cousins, and grandparents.

Turn to Joshua 2 for the story of Rahab and her family. As you read, think of her family—who might have been part of it, and how she cared for them in tragic and turbulent times. Now, putting aside her profession, picture yourself in her family position:

1. What would you have done similarly to what she did?

2. What would you have done differently?

3. When your extended family today is in trouble, how do you respond?

> To put the world right in order, we must first put the
> nation in order; to put the nation in order, we must first
> put the family in order; to put the family in order,
> we must first cultivate our personal life;
> we must first set our hearts right.
>
> CONFUCIUS

For You and Others

The other moms who gather with you for these studies are part of your family—the family of God. You probably already know that, but how often do you think of it? How often do you treat them as close family members? Work through these questions together as a family of women who are all children of God.

Read Romans 8:12-16.

1. Verses 12-15 talk about two spirits that are in opposition in believer's lives. What are those two spirits?

2. According to verse 13, what happens to those who live by the sinful nature?

3. What happens to those who live by the power of the Holy Spirit?

4. How can weak humans possibly gain victory over their sinful natures?

5. What does Paul call those who are led by the Spirit (verse 14)?

6. The New Living Translation says, "You should not be like cowering, fearful slaves. You should behave instead like God's very own children" (verse 15). How should believers *not* act? How should believers act? Describe what these opposing lifestyles would look like.

7. When are you most likely to act like a "cowering, fearful slave"?

8. When are you most likely to act like "God's very own" child?

The NIV says we can call God "*Abba,* Father" (verse 15). *Abba* is rendered "Papa" in The Message and "Father, dear Father" in the New Living Translation.

9. What affectionate name did you use for your father as a child?

10. Are you comfortable using this terminology in prayer to your heavenly Father? Why or why not?

Read Galatians 4:6-7, then Mark 14:35-36. These two passages, along with Romans 8:15, are the only places in Scripture where the name used for God is *Abba*. Compare these three passages.

11. Who calls God *Abba* in each one?

12. What sort of relationship did Jesus have with God the Father? Why do you think it would have been natural for him to call his Father *Abba?*

13. What does Jesus' use of Abba tell you about *your* use of Abba and the sort of relationship God is assuring you that you have with him?

14. What does Romans 8:16 mean when it says that God's Spirit "testifies" with your spirit?

15. How do you know that you are a child of God?

16. Spend a few minutes thinking about your own extended families and your Christian family. When you see members of your extended family, how do you recognize them? How can you recognize fellow members of God's family?

17. How do you greet members of your family? How do you greet members of your Christian family?

18. What characterizes the relationships within your family? Name several emotions as well as several actions. What characterizes relationships within God's family?

Close your time together with prayer, asking God to make you more like a family—like the fellow children of God you are.

> *This resurrection life you received from God is not a timid, grave-tending life. It's adventurously expectant, greeting God with a childlike "What's next, Papa?" God's spirit touches our spirit and confirms who we really are. We know who he is and we know who we are: Father and children.*
>
> ROMANS 8:15–16 THE MESSAGE

For You and God

Using the list you made in "For You Alone," pray in a specific way for each member of your extended family. (Be sure to include also the members of your immediate family.) Then pray for your fellow members of God's family, concentrating today on the other women in your small group. You don't need to be long-winded, but do try to be specific, bringing each family member's needs before God as you're aware of them and thanking God for each person.

Perhaps you could even commit to praying regularly (daily or weekly) for each family member. The adage "the family that prays together stays together" may be old, but it's still true. The fabric of prayer will bind your family—physical or spiritual—more closely than any other activity or emotion.

For You and Your Kids

Preschool–Lower Elementary

Make a family prayer journal together. Since most children this age can't yet read, use pictures to describe family needs. Include a page for the family as a whole, then include a page for each individual family member. Go through magazines, letting your children cut out pictures that represent family needs.

Upper Elementary–High School

Make a family prayer journal with your older children also. Again, create a page for the family as a whole, then also include a page for each individual family member. List prayer needs as well as praises on each page, noting the date you begin praying and the date your prayer is answered.

All Ages

Talk together about the importance of praying as a family, the effectiveness of bringing specific needs to God, and the significance of praising God. Help your children gain a healthy picture of God as their faithful and loving Father by noting how and when he answers your and their prayers.

session 6

you are . . . beautiful

For You Alone

You are beautiful. You are! Oh, your hair may not be cut in the latest style. Maybe your nose didn't grow (or stop growing!) to the fashionable length. Perhaps your decorating or cooking skills won't win you any awards. But you're still a beautiful, wonderful, treasured creation before the only one who really counts: God.

And don't you forget it!

To start this study on beauty, let's take a "Beautiful Bible Babes" quiz. Match each woman's description with her name:

_____ Tamar (2 Samuel 13:1)   a. Her husband called her sister instead of wife.

_____ Esther (Esther 2:17)   b. She was beautiful, but her sister had "weak eyes."

_____ Jezebel (2 Kings 9:30–33)   c. She was beautiful and smart, but her husband was a fool.

_____ Sarai [Sarah] (Genesis 12:11–13)   d. She took a bath and caught the eye of the king.

_____ Rachel (Genesis 29:17)   e. She was the beautiful daughter of King David.

_____ Bathsheba (2 Samuel 11:2–5)   f. She put on eye makeup just before she died.

_____ Abigail (1 Samuel 25:3)   g. She became queen and saved her people from death.

For You and God's Word

> *Charm is deceptive, and beauty is fleeting;*
> *but a woman who fears the LORD is to be praised.*
>
> PROVERBS 31:30

1. When is being charming a good thing? When can it be a bad thing?

2. How have you personally experienced the "fleeting" nature of beauty?

3. How does your culture treat attractive women differently from not-so-attractive women?

4. In what ways does your culture emphasize beauty over other qualities?

5. How much do good looks affect how you react to others, especially when you first meet them?

6. Why do you think so many cultures have emphasized beauty over more important qualities in women?

7. What does it mean to you to fear God?

8. How can you as a woman make fearing God rather than enhancing your physical beauty more important in your life?

9. How can you teach these vital values to your children?

> *Kindness in women, not their beauteous looks,*
> *shall win my love.*
>
> WILLIAM SHAKESPEARE, *THE TAMING OF THE SHREW*

For You and Others

1. Begin your time together with a brief discussion of beauty in today's culture:

- Name an actress you admire:
  _____

- Name an actress known for her beauty:
  _____

- Name an actress known for her talent:

  _____

- Name an actress known for her character:

  _____

2. Read Proverbs 11:22 out loud. The picture this verse presents will probably bring a smile to your faces (you're beautiful when you smile!)—or maybe even a bit of laughter. Close your eyes and spend time conjuring up a detailed picture of this pig. Go around the group, each person giving one or two words that describe the pig.

   Now close your eyes and picture what the gold ring might look like. What is incongruous and absurd about putting the two together?

3. Read Proverbs 11:22 again. What is the gold ring in a pig's snout compared to?

4. How is a gold ring in a pig's snout like a "beautiful face on an empty head" (THE MESSAGE)?

5. What does this comparison tell you about inner and outer beauty?

Read 1 Peter 3:3-6. The apostle Peter's letter to God's saints includes a comparison of outer and inner beauty. One is found to be deficient, the other valuable.

6. What sorts of things does outward beauty depend on? Include more in your answer than the three things Peter lists.

7. Which is more common today—to be known for inner beauty or for outer beauty?

8. Are the things that make a woman physically beautiful wrong? Why or why not?

9. You probably know plenty about treatments for physical beauty. What do you know about treatments for inner beauty? What would those treatments consist of? How often would they be needed in order to maintain inner beauty?

10. How does Peter describe inner beauty?

11. Do you find these characteristics attractive in other women? Why or why not?

12. Would you like these qualities to be more evident in your life? Why or why not?

Do these qualities come easily to you? Why or why not?

13. What do these verses mean for women who are naturally more ambitious? More talkative? More boisterous? Are these qualities wrong? Why or why not?

14. Over the years what will happen to outer beauty? What will happen to inner beauty?

15. Name some biblical women you admire, then try to put into words why you admire them. Did these "holy women of the past" have the inner beauty Peter describes? What about outer beauty? Does the Bible anywhere describe them as beautiful?

16. Whose daughter does verse 6 say you are? How do you become her daughter?

> The best part of beauty is that which
> no picture can express.
>
> FRANCIS BACON

For You and God

Six times in Scripture God calls his people his "treasured possession." Quickly turn to each verse and read it: Exodus 19:5; Deuteronomy 7:6; 14:2; 26:18; Psalm 135:4; Malachi 3:17. If you are a child of God, then you are one of his treasured possessions. No matter what your looks, talents, abilities—or lack of them—God treasures you because you belong to him. Pray today with a specific focus on how God made you. Thank him for the person you are, and ask him to help you become all you can be in him.

For You and Your Kids

Preschool–Middle School

Make a pig picture with your kids. Draw a large circle on a sheet of paper. Draw two ears on top and two small beady eyes. Draw another smaller circle under the eyes for the pig's snout. Take a length of another piece of paper (about 1/2 inch by 8 inches) to form the gold ring. Making two slits in the pig's snout, run the paper ring through and tape onto the back. At the bottom of your picture, write the words of Proverbs 11:22. The older your children, the more elaborate you can make your artwork.

Use the artwork as a guide to talk with (not to) your children about inner and outer beauty. Ask them questions to get them thinking about the difference and to help them want to cultivate inner beauty.

High School

Read Proverbs 11:22 together and discuss inner and outer beauty with your teens. The teen years when young persons are formulating their own special identity can be some of the most difficult in their lives. The emphasis on physical attractiveness increases with each year. The knowledge that they don't measure up becomes more and more apparent (and realistically, even the most beautiful person has flaws!). Help your teens see the fading nature of physical beauty and the lasting value of inner beauty. And in those times when it seems that they aren't listening, gently try to bring the lesson home.

leader's notes

The following notations refer to the questions in the "For You and Others" in each Bible study session. The information included here is intended to give guidance to small group leaders.

session 1:
you are . . . you

***You are a unique creation of God,
his treasured possession.***

Questions 1 and 2. If the others in the group seem hesitant to share, open the dialogue with your own thoughts from your time in "For You and God's Word." Share quickly, but honestly, giving others—by your example—encouragement to share also.

Question 3. Believing Gentiles (Paul's primary audience here) are now near God; in their former state as unbelievers, they were far away from God. According to the *NIV Bible Commentary*, "the original reference in Hebrew related to distance from Jerusalem," which in the Jewish mind was where God lived. Now, however, "near" and "far away" have primarily spiritual and only minimal physical significance.

Question 4. Through believing in the saving blood of Jesus Christ. See Ephesians 2:11.

Question 8. *Clay jars* are temporary, fragile vessels. So are we.

Question 9. The treasure is the gospel—the good news that Jesus died and rose again to save those who would turn to him in faith. The paradox between the beauty, strength, and everlasting nature of the gospel and the sinful, weak, temporal nature of its recipients (you and me!) emphasizes the fact that only God could come up with and then implement such a plan for your salvation.

session 2:
you are . . . mom

No denying it. This "you" consumes most of your energy and time. Be the best you can be at it!

Question 1. If you know of someone in your group who has struggled with the pain of infertility, ask her ahead of time if she is willing to share. If there is no one in your group who can speak personally to this topic, simply discuss together the answers to the questions.

Question 4. The priests were revered members of society in Hannah's day. They were the people's connection to God. They were God's voice in a time when no other way of hearing God existed. Therefore, their pronouncements were treated with respect and with awe.

Question 5. To remember doesn't necessitate first forgetting, at least not for God. *Remember* in this context means that God cared—that he saw Hannah's need and responded to it.

Question 6. When Hannah kept her promise, she was obeying a direct commandment of God by doing so (see Deuteronomy 23:21-23). God reveals his desire that we keep our promises by faithfully keeping his own promises to us.

Question 8. Probably about three or four. There was no way to keep milk cool and fresh in those days, so nursing provided nourishment for children until at least age three. Only then were they weaned from their mother's breast (see 1 Samuel 1:24).

session 3:
you are . . . wife

A fresh look at a much-maligned word: submission. You submit every day—to your children and their needs, to God (Jesus submitted, too), to schedules, to bosses, and to your husband.

Question 1. The Random House dictionary defines *submission* as "the act or an instance of submitting," to give over or yield to the power or authority of another. The operative word here may be *give*. Think in these terms as you try to define what submission looks like.

Question 2. Submission's tarnished image is probably due more to misuse of authority and misunderstanding than to anything else. When authority is used as a weapon, submission becomes something other than a loving act of "giving." When submission is seen as a mindless, timid, and fearful non-action rather than a self-assured choice, it becomes something no one in her right mind would want to embrace! But true submission is very different, as this study shows.

Question 5. To each other and to Christ.

Question 7. Paul calls husbands to love their wives, urging them five times to do so. While there is probably no *spiritual* significance in the number of times Paul calls men to love their wives, there is definite *actual* significance in it. In the cultural context of Paul's day, women had obligations to their husbands, but men had no obligations to their wives. Therefore, when Paul emphasizes the importance of this new way of looking at marriage—that husbands should love and care for their wives—he is raising marriage and its relationships to new and noble levels.

Question 8. Paul uses the Greek word that expresses the highest form of love—*agapē*. His view is nothing short of revolutionary:

"For a man to love his wife is to love himself. She is not to be treated as a piece of property, as was the custom in Paul's day. She is to be regarded as an extension of a man's own personality and so part of himself" *(NIV Bible Commentary).*

Question 9. Each other. Christ.

session 4:
you are ... friend

What would you do without good friends? This session emphasizes the importance of friendship in the life of a mom.

Proverbs 12:26. Cautious. Being cautious in friendships can be taken positively or negatively. Cautious people don't confide in unworthy friends. Cautious people treat friends as they would want to be treated. However, being so cautious that no close friendships are ever formed is not beneficial. Such hesitation or fear in forming close relationships can isolate you from others. So the essence of the verse is to righteously and enthusiastically form friendships, while being sure to use good sense and caution all the while.

Proverbs 16:28. Gossip. The Random House dictionary defines *gossip* as "idle talk or rumor, especially about the personal or private affairs of others." Some define gossip as passing hurtful information about someone that isn't true—but even truthful, personal information can hurt and can be defined as gossip.

Proverbs 17:9. Good friends "cover over" each other's offenses. Or, as the New Living Translation puts it, good friends disregard "another person's faults."

Proverbs 17:17. Well, of course, a good friend loves *all* the time.

Proverbs 27:6. Wounds from a friend can be trusted. "Wounds from a friend are better than many kisses from an enemy" (NLT). A friend has your best interests at heart, whereas, even when trying to show affection, an enemy doesn't. The *NIV Quest Study Bible* comments on this verse: "These [wounds] are rebukes or criticism intended to correct. Even though they are painful, they are of more use than the flattery or insincerity of an enemy. Somebody else who criticizes may be trying to harm, whereas friends do it to build up."

session 5:
you are ... family

Discover the importance of family—your immediate family as well as your extended family. They are an integral part of who you are.

Question 1. The two spirits are the spirit of a sinful nature and the spirit of righteousness, or the spirit of fear and the spirit of knowing we are children of God who don't need to be fearful.

Question 3. Only through the Holy Spirit's power. Encourage participants to discuss how they can tap into this power through prayer, through reading and knowing the Scriptures, and through close relationships with other supporting believers.

Question 5. Sons/children of God!

Question 11. Mark 14:35-36—Jesus; Romans 8:15—believers; Galatians 4:6-7—believers.

Question 13. Jesus' use of *Abba* for his Father reveals a loving and close relationship, one that encourages intimacy, no barriers, no fearful thoughts. When Paul says we have the power and the right to call the Father by such an affectionate name, he is picturing the intimate relationship God wants with us.

Question 14. "Testifies" here means God's Spirit talks with our spirit—a communication that takes place "deep in our hearts" (NLT). Encourage your group members to discuss the testifying the Spirit has done in their lives. But also encourage them to recognize that even when that sense of the Spirit's presence is absent, the truth remains. God has promised to call those who believe in him his children. This is rock-solid truth, even when we don't "feel" it.

session 6:
you are . . . beautiful

You are!
Your hair may not be cut
in the latest style. Maybe your nose isn't
the fashionable length. You may not be
the best home decorator or cook.
But you're still a beautiful, wonderful,
treasured creation before the only
one who really counts:
God.

Question 2. Pig: Fat, spotted, dirty, itchy, hairy, smelly, wet snout, beady eyes, short, stubby, fleshy.

Gold ring: Shiny, glossy, golden, sparkly, beautiful, rich.

Question 6. Think of the sorts of beauty treatments women indulge in today—manicures, spa treatments, facials, and so forth.

Question 8. Peter is not saying that outward beauty, or the frills and fripperies that go along with it, are wrong. He is simply trying to put these things into proper perspective. Women who put their emphasis there miss the more important—and lasting—benefits of inner beauty.

Question 9. Times spent building mental, physical, and spiritual health are all treatments that promote inner beauty. Reading the Bible and good books, talking to God and good friends, physical exercise—all these sorts of things work to beautify the inner person.

Question 10. A gentle and quiet spirit (1 Peter 3:4).

Question 13. These verses describe characteristics that are beautiful in any person. A self-assured, confident, and secure woman can be quiet and gentle without losing any of her strength of character. The sort of gentleness and quietness Peter has in mind are in no way to be confused with shyness or a weak meekness. Even the most ambitious and outgoing woman can have a gentleness and quietness of spirit that is her choice and her strength.

Question 15. Here's a list of several Old Testament women described as being outwardly beautiful: Sarai (Sarah), Genesis 12:11–14; Rebekah, Genesis 24:15–16; 26:7; Rachel, Genesis 29:17; Abigail, 1 Samuel 25:3; Bathsheba, 2 Samuel 11:2; Tamar (David's daughter), 2 Samuel 13:1; Tamar (Absalom's daughter), 2 Samuel 14:27; Abishag (David's nursemaid), 1 Kings 1:3–4; Vashti, Esther 1:11; Esther, Esther 2:7; Job's daughters, Job 42:15; the woman of Song of Songs.

Question 16. You become *Sarah's daughter* by doing what's right, by refusing to live fearfully but resolving to trust in God.

A Mom's Ordinary Day
Gaining and Being a Friend

Jean E. Syswerda, General Editor
Written by Jean E. Syswerda

A Bible study series addressing the unique needs of moms

No matter where you are in your life as a mom—buried in Cheerios and dirty diapers, or running the family schedule like a well-oiled machine—you need your friends. In many ways, your girlfriends are key kindred spirits, and it's their support and companionship that often gets you through the day. This Bible study explores friendship from a variety of angles, giving examples of several biblical people who were good friends, bosom buddies, soul mates. You'll examine these friendships as well as individual Scripture verses on the ups and downs of having and being a friend. Most of all, you'll learn the value of deepening your companionship with God, the one who created you to give and receive the gift of friendship.

The eight Bible studies in this series help women discover God's wisdom on how to be the best mothers, women, and disciples they can be. Each study contains six sessions divided into five flexible portions: For You Alone, For You and God's Word, For You and Others, For You and God, and For You and Your Kids. The last section helps moms share each week's nugget of truth with their children.

Softcover
ISBN: 0-310-24713-6

Pick up a copy at your favorite bookstore!

ZONDERVAN™

GRAND RAPIDS, MICHIGAN 49530 USA
WWW.ZONDERVAN.COM

A Mom's Ordinary Day

Growing Strong with God

Jean E. Syswerda, General Editor
Written by Jean E. Syswerda

A Bible study series addressing the unique needs of moms

Do you fret about what you're not instead of considering who you are in Christ? Spiritual strength doesn't come from building up your spiritual muscles. It comes from learning to rely on God's strength instead of your own, from recognizing your weaknesses and then leaning on him when you're feeling fragile. Delve into this study and discover your true source of strength. Grow strong in prayer, the Word, fellowship, and worship—and next time you're overwhelmed with whatever life has to throw at you, you'll be astonished at the power and vigor you have in God. As you work your way through this study, you'll meet God, and you'll find spiritual strength for each day.

The eight Bible studies in this series help women discover God's wisdom on how to be the best mothers, women, and disciples they can be. Each study contains six sessions divided into five flexible portions: For You Alone, For You and God's Word, For You and Others, For You and God, and For You and Your Kids. The last section helps moms share each week's nugget of truth with their children.

Softcover
ISBN: 0-310-24714-4

Pick up a copy at your favorite bookstore!

ZONDERVAN™

GRAND RAPIDS, MICHIGAN 49530 USA
WWW.ZONDERVAN.COM

A Mom's Ordinary Day
Mothering without Guilt

Jean E. Syswerda, General Editor
Written by Sharon Hersh

A Bible study series addressing the unique needs of moms

Motherhood and guilt go together like peanut butter and jelly. You feel guilty for not making organic baby food, not keeping up with your scrapbook . . . and don't forget your cluttered house. Does it ever end?

Yes, starting now. This study confronts guilt head-on. It will set your heart free to love, laugh, create, and cuddle, and to play and pray with your children. You'll meet new mentors—biblical women who model the possibilities of guilt-free mothering. As you confront your own guilt, be it over real failures or unrealistic expectations, you will find wonderful opportunities to connect with God. His love banishes all guilt and guides you into freedom in motherhood and all of life.

The eight Bible studies in this series help women discover God's wisdom on how to be the best mothers, women, and disciples they can be. Each study contains six sessions divided into five flexible portions: For You Alone, For You and God's Word, For You and Others, For You and God, and For You and Your Kids. The last section helps moms share each week's nugget of truth with their children.

Softcover
ISBN: 0-310-24715-2

Pick up a copy at your favorite bookstore!

ZONDERVAN™

GRAND RAPIDS, MICHIGAN 49530 USA
WWW.ZONDERVAN.COM

A Mom's Ordinary Day
Making Praise a Priority

Jean E. Syswerda, General Editor
Written by Ruth DeJager

A Bible study series addressing the unique needs of moms

Dishes. Laundry. Nose-wiping and boo-boo kisses. The life of a mom stretches out in predictable pattern of housework and nurturing. This Bible study will inspire you to look up from your daily work and celebrate God's presence, to become more aware of his nearness, power, and availability to you. Let this study challenge you to raise your hands in praise and worship rather than to wring them in boredom and apathy. Start using your voice to sing songs of praise rather than to grumble or complain. When you make praise a priority, you will gain a fresh perspective on the challenges you face, and you will set a new and upbeat tone for your home.

The eight Bible studies in this series help women discover God's wisdom on how to be the best mothers, women, and disciples they can be. Each study contains six sessions divided into five flexible portions: For You Alone, For You and God's Word, For You and Others, For You and God, and For You and Your Kids. The last section helps moms share each week's nugget of truth with their children.

Softcover
ISBN: 0-310-24716-0

Pick up a copy at your favorite bookstore!

ZONDERVAN™

GRAND RAPIDS, MICHIGAN 49530 USA
WWW.ZONDERVAN.COM

A Mom's Ordinary Day

Managing Your Time

Jean E. Syswerda, General Editor
Written by Erin Healy

A Bible study series addressing the unique needs of moms

What? You're too busy? Such is the life of a devoted mom—spending your day doing good things for your family, your community, and the Lord. But is your day so packed you have no time for reflection or for noticing God in the unexpected or for experiencing the joy he has built into your work as a mom, wife, and woman? Delve into this Bible study and discover the vision and purpose God has for you in the order of your days. Find out how to manage your time around that which is truly important, not just that which is good. Learn how God's generous wisdom will help you use all of your time for his glory, while taking care not to waste one precious minute.

The eight Bible studies in this series help women discover God's wisdom on how to be the best mothers, women, and disciples they can be. Each study contains six sessions divided into five flexible portions: For You Alone, For You and God's Word, For You and Others, For You and God, and For You and Your Kids. The last section helps moms share each week's nugget of truth with their children.

Softcover
ISBN: 0-310-24717-9

Pick up a copy at your favorite bookstore!

ZONDERVAN™

GRAND RAPIDS, MICHIGAN 49530 USA
WWW.ZONDERVAN.COM

A Mom's Ordinary Day

Entering God's Presence

Jean E. Syswerda, General Editor
Written by Natalie J. Block

A Bible study series addressing the unique needs of moms

As you work through this study, you will discover that God is always available to you and that you need only mustard-seed faith to move the mountains in your life. Find out how prayer can give you stamina for your daily tasks, wisdom to face your challenges, and renewed passion to walk with God. Learn effective ways to intercede for your husband, your children, your friends, and yourself. The minivan, the shower, the garden . . . anyplace can become a "prayer closet" where you can grow closer to a loving and faithful heavenly Father and find help in your time of need.

The eight Bible studies in this series help women discover God's wisdom on how to be the best mothers, women, and disciples they can be. Each study contains six sessions divided into five flexible portions: For You Alone, For You and God's Word, For You and Others, For You and God, and For You and Your Kids. The last section helps moms share each week's nugget of truth with their children.

Softcover
ISBN: 0-310-24718-7

Pick up a copy at your favorite bookstore!

ZONDERVAN™

GRAND RAPIDS, MICHIGAN 49530 USA
WWW.ZONDERVAN.COM

A Mom's Ordinary Day
Winning over Worry

Jean E. Syswerda, General Editor
Written by Jean E. Syswerda

A Bible study series addressing the unique needs of moms

Your kids. When you look at them, your heart swells with love—but sometimes with fear. Imagining the danger and horrors out there in the world just pierces a mom's heart. Worry can take away your breath, your confidence, your faith. It can even debilitate you and make you ineffective as a parent. Yet worry can be controlled. Find out how this crushing emotion can be confronted and defeated through solutions found in God's Word. Discover the peace God offers his children, and begin to win the battle over a worry-filled way of life. Learn to wield the power of prayer—your most potent weapon against fear. With help from God and his Word, you can replace worry with confident trust as you surrender to his will.

The eight Bible studies in this series help women discover God's wisdom on how to be the best mothers, women, and disciples they can be. Each study contains six sessions divided into five flexible portions: For You Alone, For You and God's Word, For You and Others, For You and God, and For You and Your Kids. The last section helps moms share each week's nugget of truth with their children.

Softcover
ISBN: 0-310-24719-5

Pick up a copy at your favorite bookstore!

ZONDERVAN™

GRAND RAPIDS, MICHIGAN 49530 USA
WWW.ZONDERVAN.COM

Women of the Bible

**A One-Year Devotional Study
of Women in Scripture**

Ann Spangler and Jean E. Syswerda

Women of the Bible focuses on fifty-two remarkable women in Scripture—women whose struggles to live with faith and courage are not unlike our own. Far from being cardboard characters, these women encourage us through their failures as well as through their successes. You'll see how God acted in surprising and wonderful ways to draw them—and you—to himself.

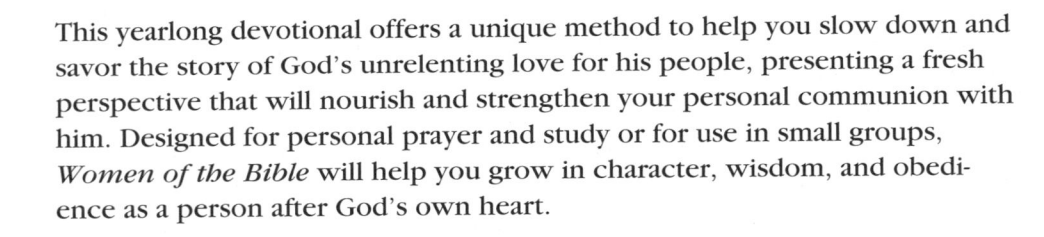

This yearlong devotional offers a unique method to help you slow down and savor the story of God's unrelenting love for his people, presenting a fresh perspective that will nourish and strengthen your personal communion with him. Designed for personal prayer and study or for use in small groups, *Women of the Bible* will help you grow in character, wisdom, and obedience as a person after God's own heart.

Hardcover 0-310-22352-0

Pick up a copy at your favorite bookstore!

ZONDERVAN™

GRAND RAPIDS, MICHIGAN 49530 USA
WWW.ZONDERVAN.COM

NIV Women of Faith Study Bible

Experience the liberating grace of God

The Bible to help Christian women experience authentic joy

God wants to fill up your days with his wonderful gift of grace and love. Let the *NIV Women of Faith Study Bible* help you remove performance-based barriers between yourself and God. Discover how women in biblical times handled struggles similar to yours; gain confidence in Christ's message of grace and freedom; and celebrate your unique, God-given womanhood. In partnership with Women of Faith, the notes and other helps in this Bible have been written specifically with today's Christian woman in mind, with the main goal of helping you experience the liberating grace of God.

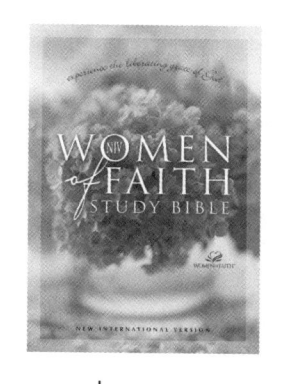

NIV — NEW INTERNATIONAL VERSION

Most read. Most trusted.

Key features of the *NIV Women of Faith Study Bible* include:

STUDY NOTES. Over 1,700 study notes shed light on the setting, meaning, and application of specific passages or themes. Over two hundred women of the past and present are quoted—from historic writers and poets such as Catherine of Siena and Elizabeth Barrett Browning to Women of Faith speakers/authors Patsy Clairmont, Barbara Johnson, Marilyn Meberg, Luci Swindoll, Sheila Walsh, and Thelma Wells.

CHARACTER SKETCHES. Full-page articles describe the challenges and opportunities of seventy-five women of the Bible. Learn from both the good and the not-so-good responses of these women to their situations and God's activity in their lives.

"ENJOYING GOD" STUDIES. For use individually or in a small group, these fifty-two studies explore key passages that reveal deep meaning and application for you as a woman today.

BOOK INTRODUCTIONS highlight the actions of the women in each book, give pertinent background information, and list all the women who appear in that book.

WOMEN IN JESUS' FAMILY TREE. God's careful selection of women in the Messianic line will inspire hope and purpose for your own life.

NEW INTERNATIONAL VERSION. Most read, most trusted translation.

COMPREHENSIVE STUDY HELPS. A concordance, center-column reference system, and color maps help you get the most out of your Bible study.

The *NIV Women of Faith Study Bible* is a guide you can trust. Filled with insight, it helps you connect with women of the past, present, and future, and it will lead you to new insight as you continue your own journey as a woman of faith.

Softcover	ISBN 0-310-91884-7	Black Bonded Leather	ISBN 0-310-92714-5
Hardcover	ISBN 0-310-91883-9	Violet Bonded Leather	ISBN 0-310-91885-5

Pick up a copy at your favorite bookstore!

ZONDERVAN™

GRAND RAPIDS, MICHIGAN 49530 USA

WWW.ZONDERVAN.COM

We want to hear from you. Please send your comments about this book to us in care of zreview@zondervan.com. Thank you.

ZONDERVAN™

GRAND RAPIDS, MICHIGAN 49530 USA
WWW.ZONDERVAN.COM